P9-CCY-224

ACKNOWLEDGMENTS

Editorial Director: Lee Kravitz

Design Director: Ellen Jacob

Creative Consultant: Cecilia Schmidt

Design Associates: Deborah Dinger, Crista Brasloff, Margaret Bruen

Illustrators: Laura Cornell (advice), Stephen Shudlich (facts)

Copy Editor: Renee Glaser

Research: Jack Silbert, Mimi George, Mi Won Kim, Margaret Stevaralgia,

Grace How, Francelia Sevin, Deborah Thompson

Special Thanks to: Kate Waters, Stuart Lewis, Jane Edgell

No part of this publication may be reproduced in whole or in part, or stored in a
retrieval system, or transmitted in any form or by any means, electronic,
mechanical, photocopying, recording, or otherwise, without written permission of the
publisher. For information regarding permission, write to Scholastic Inc.,
730 Broadway, New York, NY 10003.

ISBN 0-590-47906-7

Copyright © 1994 by Scholastic Inc.
All rights reserved. Published by Scholastic Inc.

12 11 10 9 8 7 6 5 4 3 2 1   4 5 6 7 8 9

Printed in the U.S.A   #08
First Scholastic printing, January 1994

DEAR CHELSEA

Edited by Judy Goldberg Designed by Jennifer Cole

Scholastic Inc.

New York Toronto London Auckland Sydney

Photo credits:
COVER, bkgd., Bob Lorenz; clockwise, Cynthia Johnson/Gamma Liaison; James Colburn/
Photoreporters, Inc. Back Cover, NASA; inset, Allen Tannenbaum/Sygma.

CHAPTER 1, pg. 8, Allen Tannenbaum/Sygma; pg. 10, Mark Reinstein/Photoreporters;
pg. 12, © 1991 Jim Graham/LGI; pg. 16, NASA; inset, Allen Tannenbaum/Sygma; pg. 18,
inset, AP/Wide World Photos.

CHAPTER 2, pg. 22, Bob Lorenz; pg. 24, © Harry Benson, 1993; inset, album courtesy
Electra Entertainment. Licensed by Permission. Cover photo by Peter Lerner; pgs. 26-27,
inset, Norman Isaacs/Photoreporters; Bob Lorenz; pg. 28, © Harry Benson, 1993; map
courtesy Little Rock Chamber of Commerce; inset, Harry Benson; pg. 30, top, Rick
Friedman/Black Star; bottom, United Press International Inc.; pg. 32, Reuters/Bettmann;
inset, Mark Peterson/JB Pictures; pgs. 34-35, Cecilia Schmidt.

CHAPTER 3, pg. 36, bkgd., Fred J. Maroon/Folio Inc.; inset, AP/Wide World Photos;
inset, Fred J. Maroon; pg. 38, top, Markel/Gamma Liaison; bottom, Owen D.B./Black Star;
pg. 40, bkgd., Official White House Photo; insets, clockwise from right, Culver Pictures,
Inc.; North Wind Picture Archive; Library of Congress; pg. 42, Wally McNamee/SYGMA;
inset, Official White House Photo; pg. 44, Bob Lorenz; Cynthia Johnson/Gamma Liaison;
pg. 46, bkgd., Official White House Photo; inset, United Press International Inc.;
pgs. 48-49, clockwise from left, Bettmann Archive; UPI/Bettmann; UPI/Bettmann;
AP/Wide World Photos; UPI/Bettmann; Official White House Photo/David Hume Kennerly;
Bettmann Archive, UPI/Bettmann.

CHAPTER 4, pg. 50, AP/Wide World Photos; pg. 52, Pam Price/Picture Group;
 pg. 54, Reuters/Bettmann; pg. 56, Sygma; pg. 58, Reuters/Bettmann; pg. 60, Cynthia
Johnson/Gamma Liaison; pgs. 62-63, clockwise from left, Official White House Photo;
no credit; JFK Library; Official White House Photo/BlackStar; Official White House Photo;
Leonard Lee Rue III; Library of Congress.

C O N T E N T S

9

C H A P T E R   O N E

I Know Just How You Feel

C H A P T E R   T W O   **23**

Fan Mail

37   C H A P T E R   T H R E E

Life in the White House

C H A P T E R   F O U R   **51**

Socks

INTRODUCTION

Dear Reader,

I am writing to you from a room filled with letters. Love letters, like-you-a-lot letters, funny letters, letters filled with advice, just-want-to-say-hi! letters, thousands upon thousands of letters — more than 12,000 of them! And each and every one of them is for Chelsea Clinton, the daughter of the President of the United States of America. They were written by someone who is probably just like you: a person under the age of 18 who is psyched beyond belief to have one of their own living in that big white house.

These letters came to my office because I'm an editor at Scholastic Magazines. A while ago, we asked our readers to write to Chelsea and we said we'd pass those letters on to her. We also said that we would publish the best ones in our magazines. The letters were so great, though, that we decided to put them together in a book — the one you are holding in your hands right now.

Oh, but this book is not just letters to Chelsea. It also has every little thing you would ever want to know about your favorite First Kid, and of course, Socks. It has snippets of advice, cool pictures, and fun facts galore.

Now, it's time for me to pass all these letters on to Chelsea, and pass this book on to you. If after you're done reading you want to write to Chelsea yourself, or to her Mom or President-Dad, the address is: The White House, 1600 Pennsylvania Avenue, W Washington, DC 20500.

Have fun!

Sincerely,

Judy

Judy Goldberg

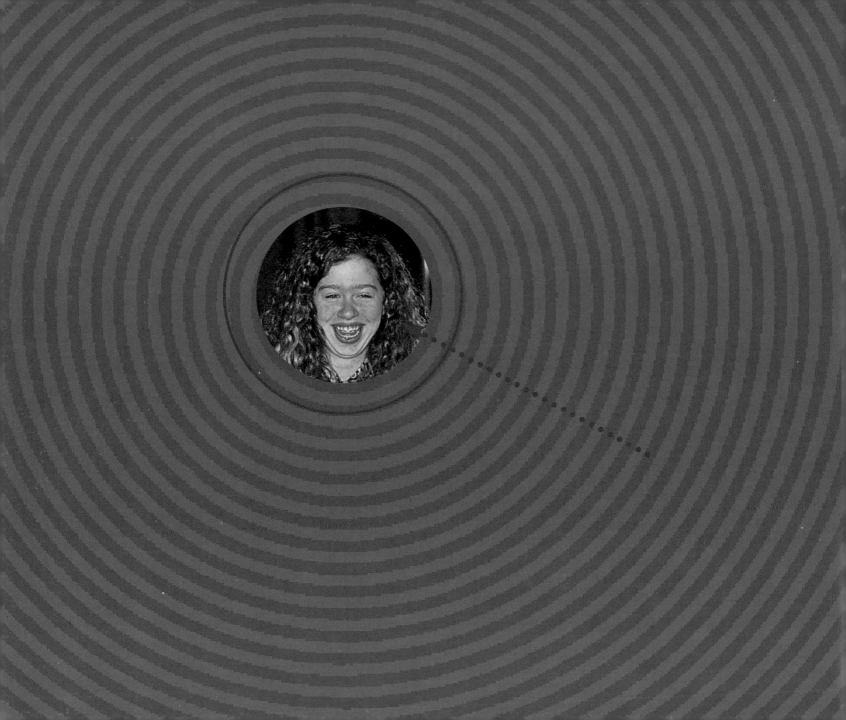

I Know Just How

You
Feel

CHAPTER ONE

Fact

Secret
Service
agents
accompany
Chelsea
everywhere.
They have
their own
office on
the third
floor of
Chelsea's
school and
they sit on
bleachers
during her
soccer
practice.

Dear Chelsea,

Hi! My name is Katie! I know just how you feel. My dad was the **mayor** of the town where I live, Blasdell. I always got **bugged** by someone no matter where I went! Isn't it **annoying**?! It drove me **crazy**! People were always saying, "Oh! Are you the mayor's daughter?" I didn't want my dad to be the mayor anymore. I mean, I was **happy** for him, but I didn't like it. Is that the way you **feel**?

Well, I'm sure it will all work out for you.

Yours Truly,
Katie McGuire
Blasdell, New York

Try going with your dad everywhere and spend time with him while he's working. I learned how to put an addition on our house from hanging out with my dad. Think about what you could learn, from the President, your dad.

— *Philip Zigler, San Jose, CA*

F**act**

12

Chelsea's
favorite
music
group is
Boyz II
Men.

Dear Chelsea,

Hello, I live in Hyattsville, Maryland, and I know how you feel. It's pretty bad to have cameras all over you. It would be very annoying.

I'm not exactly **Mr. Ordinary**. For starters, I play for a band that plays somber **music** such as my favorite group, The Cure. For some reason I like the group. I have 12 of their tapes too. They're not all I listen to, though. I like The Sundays, Soup Dragons, Kitchens of Distinction, and **10,000 Maniacs**.

I'm in the eighth grade, going on 14 years old. My life was pretty good until my **girlfriend** and I broke up. Luckily, I got over it quickly.

My only advice is to talk about stuff with someone or start a journal. It's always good to talk to people to get your mind off of things.

Stay Calm!

> Your friend,
> Jacob Reid
> Hyattsville, Maryland

The most sneaky way to handle the press would be to ask your father's advisers if they have any gossip on certain reporters, and the next time they bother you, tell the gossip on camera in front of their face. —Raymond Carlos, Azusa, CA

Dear Chelsea,

My name is Kay and I'm a normal teenager just like you. I know you probably don't feel very **normal**, but I'm sure that you still have the same confusion and **emotions** as every other girl that's changing. On top of it all, you have an added responsibility— you're always in the spotlight.

I understand if you're **tired** of smiling all the time or having people act as if they know you, when really they don't know the first thing about the **real** you at all. Everybody knows your face, but the real Chelsea is just **dying** to bust out.

You have to try to be as normal as possible. It might be hard for people to get past the fact that your dad is the **President**—who can blame them—but you'll still make true **friends**. The ones who know the real Chelsea, the ones who really care, are going to last a lifetime.

Still, becoming the President's **daughter** carries a lot of responsibilities with it. You still have to get along with people you might not like, be courteous and

Fact

Chelsea's
only fault,
according
to her dad:
She stays
up too late.

14

ladylike, and spend a lot of your free time in boring places that you don't want to be. When your **father** took the **oath** of office, so did you. Whether you like it or not, it's your job too and you're stuck with it. Don't rebel, make this a once-in-a-lifetime **experience** and get the most from it. Most of all, understand what your dad is going through. He's in the spotlight much more than you. Think of all the **pressure!** Just be there for him and let him know that you're with him, no matter what the tabloids say.

Your supporting friend,
Kay Baker
Fort Worth, Texas

I just got my first zit. Have you tried Clearasil? Well, it really works. And another thing, my friend Ryan was elected Junior Vice President and he's become snotty, but don't let that get to you. —Jonathan S. Comish, Baton Rouge, LA

NEVER SEEN ONE LIKE IT.

WOW, LOOK AT THAT ZIT.

OH, POOR DEAR

Fact

When
Chelsea
grows up
she wants
to be a
scientist
or an
astronaut—
or both.

When you get older you should become a police officer. At least then you wouldn't have so many people on you.

—Raymond Carlos, Azusa, CA

Dear Chelsea,

My name is Alana Wilson. I go to Lake Dolloff Elementary, in Washington State. I'm in fifth grade, and overjoyed about writing to Chelsea. I've been the daughter of someone very important many, many times, and sometimes it's not very fun. My mom is a manager at Boeing in Seattle, and on weekends when I go to work with her, if she's not with me she sends an employee from the third floor to watch over me — kinda like a bodyguard. But I just grin and bear it, thinking to myself, "It'll be over soon," and try not to complain. 'Cause I want to stay irresponsible until they start piling the jobs on me!!

Sincerely,
Alana Wilson
Auburn, Washington

18

Fact

Chelsea's favorite activity is ballet.

Dear Chelsea,

I heard about people making fun of you. I know how you feel. People used to make fun of me because I was **big** and **tall**. Just ignore them! I found out people were calling me names just for a **laugh**. They laughed because I would get upset and sometimes cry. The next day when they called me a name I didn't get **upset**. They stopped calling me **names** because they didn't get their laughs anymore.

Sincerely,
David Noles
Lynchburg, Tennessee

P.S. Don't worry about your **braces.** I've got braces too. I also wanted to tell you you're very pretty.

Sometimes when I go out and don't want anyone to see how upset I am, I just imagine the funniest thing possible. Such as someone getting their hair stuck in a pencil sharpener. This cheers me up. The best of luck. —L. McLeary, Redondo Beach, CA

Who You Are!

- Total number of kids in America: **72.4 million**

- Number of only kids: **13.3 million**

- Average number of times a 14–year–old has moved: **2**

- Number of kids attending public school in 1993: **43 million**

- Number of kids attending private school in 1993: **5.4 million**

- Total number of households with cats: **62.4 million**

- Average number of cats per house: **2**

- Percentage of 4–to–17–year–olds who have their own TV set: **40**

- Number of 12–to–18–year–olds with braces: **5 million**

- Average monthly allowance for 12–to–18–year–olds: **$35**

- Amount kids spent of their own money on snacks and toys: **$62 billion**

- Favorite food among teenagers: **Pizza**

- Percentage of 12–to–19–year–olds who have their own phone: **58.1**

Fan Mail

C H A P T E R   T W O

Fact

Chelsea was named after the folk song "Chelsea Morning," written by Joni Mitchell and recorded by Judy Collins in 1969.

Dear Chelsea,

Hi, this is Dennis Grijalva and I'm 13 years old and I really **like** you. I'm not saying I like **you** because you're the President's daughter, but I'm saying I like you because of who you are. I don't think it is **nice** that people are making **fun** of you and I wanted you to know that I'll be next to you all the way.

I was hoping that maybe your dad will pay for a plane and maybe I could **meet** you in real life and stay a couple of days at the White House!

There's a lot of kids **joking** around but I'm **serious**. I want to know if you will go out with me. Will you please write back and tell me your **answer** about me going out with you, and **me** meeting you in the White House?

Well, Better Go,
Dennis Grijalva
Taft, California

P.S. Don't forget to write back. **Thanks.**

Dating: I think you should date if you like, but when you're dating a boy, make sure he's not dating you for your money. Well, I gotta jet. —Kenya Tillman, Marshville, NC

Fact

Chelsea's favorite foods are broccoli and macaroni and cheese. She also loves fried chicken, baked potatoes, chocolate cake, and Mexican food.

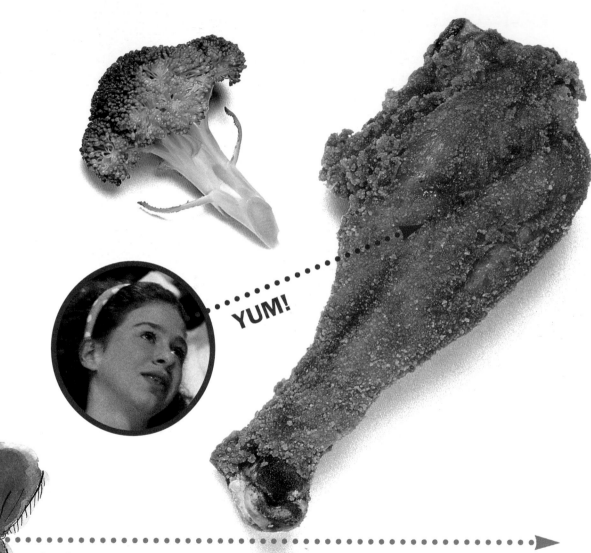

YUM!

*As for politics: **DON'T GET INVOLVED!** As for friends: I recommend you make some so you can play hide-and-seek in that huge house. And as for dating: I think that is none of my business at all. I don't think I even want to know your choice in that area.* —Kevin Rieder, Hawthorn Woods, IL

Ms. Clinton,

   As soon as I heard your father became President I was so **happy**.
I think your father's plans for the **future** are very good. You are
lucky to have a father like Mr. Clinton, and Mr. Clinton
is lucky to have a daughter like you. I really would like to meet you
and your father and mother — especially you. Because you're very
beautiful. You probably hear that a lot, though.

   Let me tell you about myself. I'm a **cowboy**. I like to ride bulls in
rodeos. I like to wrestle in school. I like to work on cars and do models
of cars.

   I don't do anything like drugs or drink. I would like to meet you,
maybe even take you out to eat or to the movies. I could come up there
to D.C. because my cousin is coming to D.C. this spring for a contest.
By the way, I love to draw and do **impressions**. I'm not a nasty or
skuzzy person. My ego isn't high. I don't think I'm perfect. I think
I'm a normal person.

   Love,
   Travis Ketchum
   Carthage, Missouri

P.S. Please write back or call.

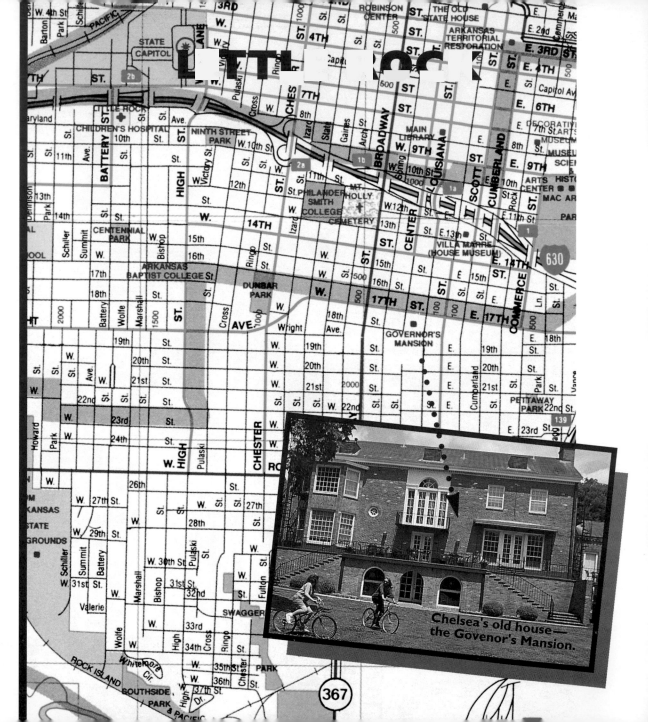

LITTLE ROCK

Fact

Chelsea was born on February 27, 1980, in Little Rock, Arkansas. Her sign is Pisces.

Chelsea's old house— the Govenor's Mansion.

Dear Chelsea,

I'm Todd W. Walker, one of your **biggest** fans. I bet it's pretty **cool** to be the most famous kid in the United States. I would love to be your brother. Your **dad** is pretty cool. And your **mom** is the prettiest First Lady I have ever seen. Well, I have to go . . . bye.

Sincerely,
Todd Walker
Newberry, South Carolina

P.S. I do believe in a place called **Hope.***

*Hope is the small town where Chelsea's dad grew up.

Is it scary being the President's daughter? *If you are scared I would tell someone, but if you've already told someone, I suggest that you go bug a Secret Service agent. It'll take your mind off things.*

— James Steele, Arlington, VA

Chelsea's House

Fact

Yes, Chelsea is allowed to have slumber parties.

Dear Chelsea,

My name is Danielle. I am 10 years old. I live in Indian Head, Maryland. I am in **fifth** grade. My dad works for your dad. He is a member of the Explosive Ordnance Disposal team. He works alongside the U.S. Secret Service providing security. I have always wanted to **sleep** in the White House, so do you think your dad would let you have a **slumber party**? My dad has offered to take off work and provide the security. I would love to meet you and your family, not to mention **Socks**. I don't have a **cat** but I do have two **dogs**. A cocker spaniel and a rottweiler. I also have a sister. Her name is Elizabeth. She is 5.

Well, I have to go. I would really appreciate it if you would write or call. I am glad I got the chance to write you and to ask you the one question that my dream is. Well, gotta go. **Bye**.

Sincerely,
Danielle Ditsch
Indian Head, Maryland

Do you get to have friends over? *If you don't, ask politely and give sad puppy eyes.*
—David Dokman, Millington, MI

Fact

Chelsea's favorite subjects in school are science and math. Her favorite sports are soccer and volleyball.

Dear Chelsea,

My name is Connie Lynn Youngs. I am 12 years old. I'm **deaf**. I like your dad. I watched President Clinton **sign** on TV. He signed ✋ (I love you). I know how to **sign**. Do you know how to sign?

My favorite class is science. My favorite sports are **baseball**, **basketball**, and **volleyball**.

I saw you in the newspaper. You were pretty. Are you **happy** because you get new friends? You should bring old friends to the White House. Did you move with your **cat**?

Write back please, Chelsea.

> Your friend,
> Connie Lynn Youngs
> Clayton, New York

I have some advice for you, don't take any. You'll never learn anything about life if you take other people's advice. You'll just be living their lives. Just because you're the First Kid, doesn't mean now you need a second personality. You know what I mean?

— Stephanie Jordan, Montgomery, NY

CHELSEA ARMY & NAVY

HOTEL CHELSEA

CHELSEA

CHELSEA FISH MARKET

CHELSEACLINTON Cafe

CHELSEA CLINTON NEWS

CHELSEA GYM

Chelsea is a section of New York City.

Life in the
White House

CHAPTER THREE

School

Going Home

Fact

On a typical day, Chelsea returns to the White House after school, eats a snack, talks on the phone with friends, does her home-work, and eats dinner with her family at 7:30 or 8:00 p.m.

Dear Chelsea,

Hi! My name is Alex Harris. I am **lucky** to have both my parents at home. I have three very **dangerous** dogs that protect my home. Right now I'm only 11 years old. I am very proud of my age.

For about 20 seconds I am going to tell you how old my **dogs** are in dog **years**. My biggest dog is still living and he is 35 years old. My second biggest dog is 28 years old, and my **smallest** dog is only 21 years old.

I have always wanted to know what it's like to live in the White House. If I could live in the White House I would go to every room in it. Is it true that in the kitchen there are over 3,000 types of **chocolates**? Also, is it true that the servants have to watch you even when you take a **shower**? There is one more thing that I would like to know: Have you gotten lost yet in the White House?

I wanted to tell you how good I think you are with other children. I have seen some good role **models** in my life, but you, you beat every one of them.

Your friend,
Alex Harris
Houston, Texas

I'd love to live in the White House, but if I were you I'd try not to get too addicted to it because one day you might have to move back to Arkansas or some other place. —Jon Biderman, Valley Stream, NY

Fact

There are 132 rooms in the White House and 32 bathrooms. Some people think that Abraham Lincoln's ghost haunts the White House.

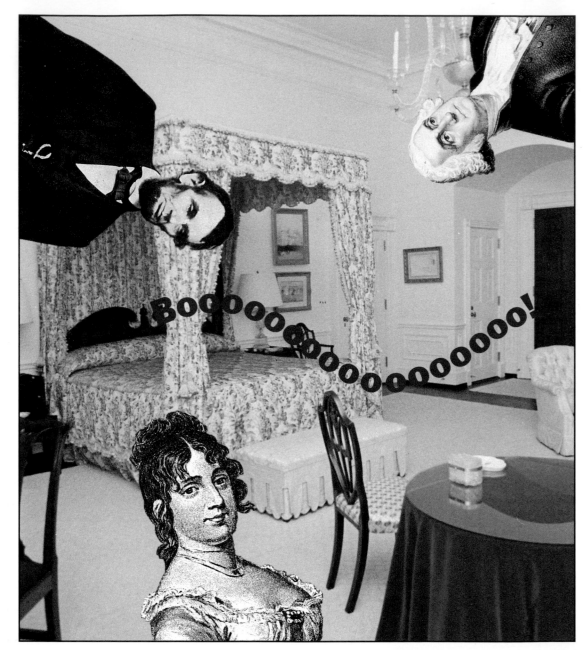

Dear Chelsea,

How does it feel to be a President's kid? I hope you don't change just because you're **famous**.

My brother read a book about the White House. It said that there have been sightings of the **ghosts** of Abraham Lincoln, George Washington, and Dolley Madison in the White House. Have you seen them lately? They aren't mean. Abraham Lincoln always **knocks** before entering a room.

> Your friend,
> Kim Taylor
> Nixa, Missouri

P.S. What was your most **embarrassing** moment? I won't tell anyone. You have my word.

Let me give you some advice: Never chew gum when you're sleeping because it could go in your hair. And Chelsea, I've got to tell you something. I heard that Abraham Lincoln haunts the White House. I hope that is not true.

—Aenoy Ratsaphouh, Wausau, WI

The White House library

F
act

In the
White House,
Chelsea has
a little room
for studying.
She can also
do her
homework
in the
Presidential
study next to
the Oval
Office, and
use the
White House
library, which
has about
2,600 books.

Dear Chelsea,

If I were you and in your position, I would talk to your dad about giving **kids** rights. They are human beings like **adults**.

When kids are told they're **wrong**, they don't want **yelling** or **punishing**. They just want a friend to lean on. Kids are little people wanting big people to like them. And they should have rights too.

Sincerely,
Angel Baker
Newberry, South Carolina

As America's new First Kid, try to be smart and love your country. Try to look your best, don't take drugs, eat healthy foods, be nice to everybody, including your elders, don't be mean to poor people, and get out and see the scenery in Washington.

—Nicholas Denham, Chattanooga, TN

GO TO THE HEAD OF THE CLASS.

GRADE 6
GRADE 5
GRADE 4
GRADE 3
GRADE 2

Chelsea

68 69 70
58 59
56 47 48
45
34 35 36 37
23 24 25 26

44

F
act

Chelsea was smart enough to skip third grade.

Don't listen to anyone. Your parents cannot make 250 million people happy. Someone will always be complaining.
—Thomas L. Richardson, Richmond, VA

Dear Chelsea,

Since you are the First Kid, and your father is the President, I would start a Kids Vote Club. It should allow kids to vote on important topics concerning our country. It might be a very important step to show adults that kids really do care about our country. Also, it might make some kids feel more important.

In this club you should have weekly meetings that should be televised. People from all over could watch the meetings. Also, you should give out free prizes to your members. Another thing the club could do would be to have fund-raisers all over the country.

This club should have a president (you), who should have a secretary to record or explain any complications. The secretary should be chosen by the president, to serve until a new election is called. There should also be a vice president, who is chosen by vote every 6 months. There also should be a congress of 12 people chosen yearly. The congress should represent the people in small arguments that can be decided by a simple vote. In larger arguments, the entire club should vote on a decision.

Your Suggestioner,
Ben Davis
Saranac, New York

P.S. I think you should have your father upgrade your allowance to $24,000 a year and send half of it to me.

Fact

The White House has a bowling alley, movie theater, swimming pool, gym, game room, putting green, horseshoe pit, and new jogging track.

Dear Chelsea,

What's it like being the most known girl in the United States of America?

I am no good at **sports** but everybody says I am. Especially basketball— I'm tellin' ya, I stink! I am average at **baseball** and **soccer**. I put a notch on my bat every time I hit a home run. So far I don't have any notches on it.

How do ya feel about having **Secret Service** men following you around all the time with semiautomatic guns in their coats?

Sincerely,
Jeremy Gray
Louisville, Kentucky

P.S. Would you send me a picture of you?

NOT THERE...
NOT THERE...
NOT THERE...

I feel sorry for you, because I really wouldn't want somebody following me everywhere I go. I think you should handle this like I handle my brother— just don't think they are there. —Eric Swain, El Cajon, CA

Willie

1861-1865 **Willie, 10, and Tad Lincoln, 7**
Dad: Abraham Lincoln
Generally mischievous, Willie and Tad once shocked guests by riding a goat through the White House drawing room.

1901-1909
Alice, 17, Theodore Jr., 12, Kermit, 11, Ethel, 8, Archie, 7, and Quentin Roosevelt, 3
Dad: Theodore Roosevelt
Archie and Quentin once took a giant snowball to the White House balcony and dumped it on their dad and a guest as they left the building. When it wasn't snowing, Quentin could be found walking on stilts in the White House flower beds.

Far left, Mom Julia; second from left, Dad; third from right, Jesse

1869-1877

Jesse Root Grant, 11
Dad: Ulysses S. Grant
Jesse started a secret White House club complete with 75 members, a club-house, and a newspaper.

Esther

1885-1889 — 1893-1897

Ruth, 1, and Esther Cleveland
Dad: Grover Cleveland
The Baby Ruth candy bar was named after Ruth. Esther was the first and only baby born in the White House.

Left to right: Quentin, Dad, Theodore Jr., Archie, Alice, Kermit, Mom Edith, Ethel

1977-1981

Amy Carter, 9
Dad: Jimmy Carter
At state dinners, Amy brought her books to the table and read.

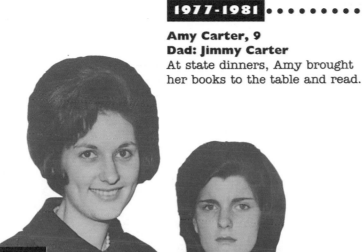

Dad, John Jr.

Lynda Bird

Luci Baines

Amy

1961-1963

Caroline, 3, and
John F. Kennedy Jr., 2 months
Dad: John F. Kennedy
John-John liked to spend his days playing under his dad's desk in the Oval Office.

1963-1969

Lynda Bird, 19, and
Luci Baines Johnson, 16
Dad: Lyndon B. Johnson
Lynda used to read her dad's speeches and grade them "A," "B," or "C." Luci explained, "You have to be pushy to have any friends at the White House. No one will call you anymore. You have to call them."

Left to right: Susan, Steve, Mom Betty, Jack, Dad, Mike & wife Gayle

1974-1977

Mike, 24, Jack, 22, Steve, 18, and Susan Ford, 17
Dad: Gerald R. Ford
Jack brought former Beatle George Harrison over for lunch. Steve avoided the White House by working on a ranch in Montana — but 10 Secret Service agents went with him. Susan invited her entire high school class to the White House for their senior prom.

Socks

C H A P T E R   F O U R

Fact

Socks was a stray kitten when Chelsea found him. He was probably born some-time in July 1990.

Dear Chelsea,

I am 10 years old and I am in the 5th grade. I live in Arlington, Virginia, in a little house with my mom.

How is Socks doing? I am a cat **lover**, so I always focus in on the **news** when they show Socks or do reports on him. I have two cats myself, **Tygr** (pronounced Tigger) and **Ozzy**. I know how cats can be great company. Ozzy is crazy, wild, and really fast. Tygr, my other cat, is really, really slow, fat, and **sleeps** all day.

Sincerely,
Jesse Panneton
Arlington, Virginia

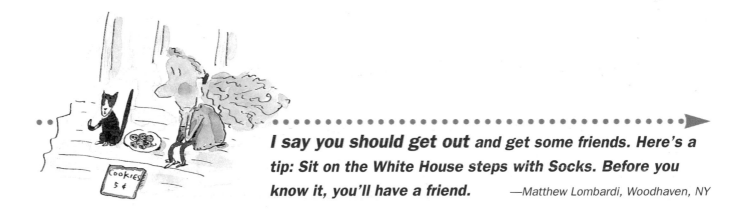

I say you should get out and get some friends. Here's a tip: Sit on the White House steps with Socks. Before you know it, you'll have a friend. —Matthew Lombardi, Woodhaven, NY

Fact

Socks is very well-behaved, and according to Chelsea, "Basically, he can go wherever he wants."

Dear Socks,

How are you? How's life in the White House? Can we come live with  you? I'm sure we could help you ruin the furniture— scratch it we mean. Believe us, we're good at that. Do you have a **girlfriend**? What's her name? Do you love Chelsea? We **love** our owners.

We think you are lucky to live in the White House. We would die to live there in that big house. Oh yeah, where do you **sleep**? Do you like the outside? We do, but we're house cats. Sometimes we sneak out, but then we get in **trouble**. Do you ever get lost? Do you climb trees? Do you **wander** around the neighborhood, or just the yard? Do you have a big yard? How old are you? We are 2 years old in people years. Are you the family cat? We are. Were you **declawed**? We weren't. Are you a crafty cat? Do you jump on the counter and the table and the places that you aren't allowed to be? We do and our owners hate it. **Hee, hee, hee.**

Love,
Ody and Cotton—that's us.
(As told to Lillian and Sarah Dunlap
Brooklyn, New York)

MY Technique

***Socks, scratch all the furniture** in the White House! I bet they would **record that on the news and you would be famous.** —Sonya Goddy, Brooklyn, NY*

F act

Socks sleeps in the office of the White House's head usher, Gary Walter, or in Chelsea's bedroom.

Dear Chelsea,

Hi. How are you? I am fine. You are very **pretty**, and you're only one year older than me.

I heard this and maybe it's not true, but a boy in my classroom said your cat was getting a brass **bed**, **spa**, and his own **room**.

I know you're probably wondering what I look like? I have brownish-blond **curly** hair and hazel eyes. I'm tall. Sometimes I wear **glasses**.

Sincerely,
Amanda Connor
Mt. Savage, Maryland

P.S. You're my idol.

*Here is a tip. **Don't let Socks in the Lincoln bedroom. It may be haunted.** —Laura Chan, Cape Coral, FL*

Fact

Socks wears a red jeweled collar. When he leaves the White House, Socks is led around on an extremely long leash.

Dear Socks,

I wish that you would look on your four-year term as First Cat of America with care. I hope you can make the American people think about **humane** pet-care projects. Also,  I think you should set up a good reputation for American dogs, cats, fish, **turtles**, and other animals.

It would not be fun to be in your **paws**, with all your responsibilities and **duties**. I have a few questions to ask. Do you like any other cats? Does Chelsea take good care of you? I would if you were my cat. Do you have any **idols** like Benji the dog?

Sincerely,
Eric Newman
Sylvania, Ohio

Spend a lot of time with your cat. Feed it, water it, and pet it a lot, so it doesn't get too close to your servants and will still pay attention to you. —Craig Knight, Louisville, KY

Fact

Chelsea's
mom and
dad are
allergic to
Socks.

Dear Socks,

How is life in the White House? I heard the caviar is really **purrfect** there.

How is your **mistress**, Chelsea, taking these new changes in her life? She must be pretty happy her dad is the President of America. Going to a private school won't be so bad. At least it will cut down on the stress of people **flocking** around her. It will be hard to have **privacy** with her friends, with the media and reporters on her tail. But still, she has the White House to live in—the most popular and almost the biggest home in America. While she is dealing with these changes, give her a lot of **kitty** attention and kitty **kisses** and cuddles.

> Love,
> Rum, Tum, and Tugger
> c/o Phedre vonKallenbach
> Gig Harbor, Washington

P.S. Let's be kitty cat pen pals. Write.

I think you should buy a puppy and name it Shoes.

—Arthur J. Klein, San Francisco, CA

President:
Theodore Roosevelt

Pets:

1 bear named Jonathan Edwards.

1 lizard named Bill.

5 guinea pigs named Admiral Dewey, Dr. Johnson, Bishop Doane, Fighting Bob Evans, and Father O'Grady.

1 pig named Maude.

1 badger named Josiah.

1 blue macaw named Eli Yale.

1 hen named Baron Spreckle.

1 rabbit named Peter.

1 rat named Jonathan.

4 dogs named: Algonquin Jack, Skip, Pete, and Manchu.

1 snake named Emily Spinach.

1 one-legged rooster

1 hyena

1 barn owl

2 kangaroo rats

1 flying squirrel

Theodore Jr., with Eli Yale.

President Woodrow Wilson's flock of sheep.

Animal House
A guide to some former first pets

President:
John F. Kennedy
Pets:
2 deer

1 cat
named Tom Kitten.

2 hamsters
named Billy and Debbie.

2 parakeets
named Bluebelle and Maybelle.

1 canary
named Robin.

9 dogs —
Charlie, Clipper, Shannon, Wolf, Butterfly, White Tips, Blackie, Streaker, and Pushinka (who was the daughter of Stelka, one of the first dogs in space).

3 horses
named Sardar, Leprechaun, and Tex.

1 pony called Macaroni.

President Warren Harding's pet turkey.

President: Gerald R. Ford
Pets: 1 cat named Chan. **1 dog** named Liberty. One night after taking Liberty for a walk at 3 a.m., President Ford got locked out of the White House. He had to pound on the door until the Secret Service let him back in.

President: George Bush
Pet: 1 dog named Millie, who wrote a best-selling book.